Pre-Printing Fun

Developmentally-Appropriate Activities that will Strengthen Fine Motor Skills, Improve Eye-Hand Coordination, and Increase Pencil Control

by
Sherrill B. Flora

illustrated by
Julie Anderson

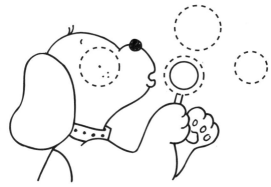

Publisher
Key Education—An imprint of Carson-Dellosa Publishing LLC
Greensboro, North Carolina

CONGRATULATIONS ON YOUR PURCHASE OF A KEY EDUCATION PRODUCT!

The editors at Key Education are former teachers who bring experience, enthusiasm, and quality to each and every product. Thousands of teachers have looked to the staff at Key Education for new and innovative resources to make their work more enjoyable and rewarding. Key Education is committed to developing and publishing educational materials that will assist teachers in building a strong and developmentally appropriate curriculum for young children.

PLAN FOR GREAT TEACHING EXPERIENCES WHEN YOU USE
EDUCATIONAL MATERIALS FROM KEY EDUCATION PUBLISHING COMPANY, LLC

Credits
Author: Sherrill B. Flora
Creative Director: Annette Hollister-Papp
Illustrator: Julie Anderson
Editor: George C. Flora
Production: Key Education Staff
Cover Photo Credits: © Shutterstock.com

Key Education welcomes manuscripts and product ideas from teachers.
For a copy of our submission guidelines, please send a self-addressed, stamped envelope to:

Key Education Publishing Company, LLC
Acquisitions Department
PO Box 35665
Greensboro, NC 27425-5665

Standard Book Number: 978-1-602680-23-4
Pre-Printing Fun
Key Education—An imprint of Carson-Dellosa Publishing LLC
Copyright © 2008 by Carson-Dellosa Publishing Company, LLC
Greensboro, North Carolina 27425

01-135118091

Contents

INTRODUCTION 4

STUDENT CHECK LIST ....:5

STRAIGHT LINES 6–16
  Let's learn how to draw a tall straight line................6
  Color Crayons/Letter "I"...7
  Match the "Same" Pictures/Letter "i"...................8
  Let's learn how to draw a long straight line.............9
  Help the Cat Get Back Home/
    Letters "L" and "T"..10
  Kites in the Sky/Letter "t"..................................11
  Dot-to-Dot City/Letters "F" and "E"....................12
  Copy Cat Letters/Letters "H" and "I"..................13
  Graphing Picture House/Review..........................14
  Trace and Color Squares/Draw Squares...............15
  Trace and Color Rectangles/
    Draw Rectangles...16

SLANTED LINES 17–31
  Let's learn how to draw an "up" slanted line.........17
  Let's learn how to draw a "down" slanted line.........18
  Finish the Feathers/Letters "V" and "v"...............19
  Finish the Picture/Letters "W" and "w"................20
  Help the Bird Get to Her Nest/Letter "N"...............21
  The Mountain Man/Letter "M" 22
  Zig-Zag Goals!/Letter "Z" and "z"......................23
  My Own Tree House/Review 24
  Snowflakes/Letters "X" and "x".........................25
  Party Hats/Letter "A" 26
  "Y" Guys/Letters "Y" and "y"............................27
  Singing Chicks/Letters "K" and "k".....................28
  Graphing Picture Castle/Review 29
  Trace and Color Triangles/Draw Triangles............30
  Trace and Color Rhombus'/Draw Rhombus' 31

CIRCLES 32–37
  Let's learn how to draw a circle 32
  Blowing Bubbles/Letters "O" and "o" 33
  Barnyard Chicks/Letter "Q".................................34
  Trace and Color Circles/Draw Circles..................35
  Trace and Color Ovals/Draw Ovals 36
  Cut and Paste Puzzle/Challenge Activity..............37

CURVES 38–62
  Let's learn how to draw a left ear stroke 38
  Finish the Animals/Letters "C" and "c".................39
  Leaping Lily Pads!/Letter "G"..............................40
  Ladybugs Everywhere!/Letter "e"........................41
  Long and Short Legs/Letters "a" and "d".............42
  Kittens and Yarn/Letters "g" and "q".....................43
  Finish the Picture/Review...................................44
  Let's learn how to draw a right ear stroke..............45
  Under the Sea/Letter "D".....................................46
  Penguin's Hidden Pictures/Letters "P" and "R".......47
  Following Directions/Letter "B"............................48
  Finish the Owl/Letters "p" and "b"......................49
  Trace and Dot-to-Dot/Review.............................50
  Slithering Snakes/Review....................................51
  Flamingos/Letters "S" and "s"............................52
  Let's learn how to draw a smile stroke...................53
  The Wavy Ocean/Letters "U" and "u"...................54
  Cute Cottage Dot-to-Dot/Letters "J" and "j" 55
  Flower Garden/Review..56
  Let's learn how to draw a frown stroke..................57
  Hopping Critters/Letters "n" and "m"....................58
  Following Directions/Letters "r" and "h"................59
  Puppy's Hidden Picture/Letter "f".........................60
  A Tricky Maze/Review 61
  Finish the Peacock/Review..................................62

PRACTICE PRINTING THE ALPHABET 63

STANDARDS CORRELATION 64

SEQUENCE OF WHEN LETTERS ARE INTRODUCED

tall and long straight lines									slanted lines			
I	i	L	T	t	F	E	H	I	V	v	W	w

slanted lines continued										circles	
N	M	Z	z	X	x	A	Y	y	K	k	O	o

circles	left ear curves							right ear curves			
Q	C	c	G	e	a	d	g	q	D	P	R	B

right ear curves con't	left & right ear curves		smiling curves				frowning curves			
p	b	S	s	U	u	J	j	n	m	r	h	f

Introduction

Learning how to print can either be a frustrating and challenging experience for a young child, or it can be a fun and successful experience. All the activities in *Pre-Printing Fun* have been designed to make learning how to print a successful experience.

So, what makes the difference? Often, teachers and parents present learning how to print letters in alphabetical sequence. Developmentally, this makes very little sense. Children need to learn how to control a pencil and how to make various handwriting strokes before they are able to print letters. *Pre-Printing Fun* gives children the opportunity to learn how to control a pencil and then learn specific handwriting strokes, which then enables them to print a variety of alphabet letters. For example, in *Pre-Printing Fun* children are taught first how to make "tall straight lines" and then "long straight lines." When children are able to print these lines they are then able to print "l, i, L, t, T, F, E, H, and I. Children immediately feel successful and are learning correct handwriting skills.

The strokes taught in *Pre-Printing Fun* are as follows:

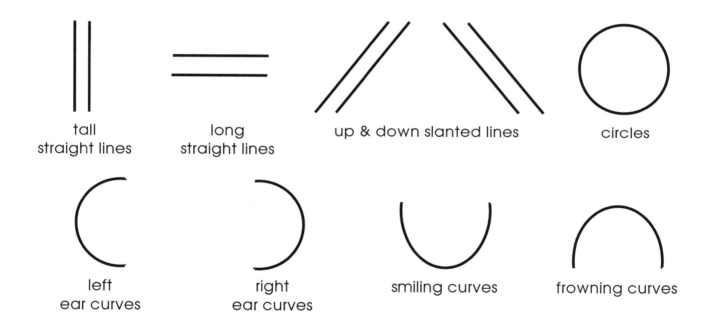

| tall straight lines | long straight lines | up & down slanted lines | circles |

| left ear curves | right ear curves | smiling curves | frowning curves |

EXTRA IDEAS TO STRENGTHEN FINE MOTOR SKILLS

Children need a large variety of experiences to strengthen fine motor skills and to learn how to print. Finger painting, modeling with play dough, opening and closing clothes pins, using scissors and snipping the edges of paper, peg boards, and beading are all wonderful activities that will build small muscle strength and coordination.

Student Check List

Name_____ **Date** _____

1. The student has mastered the following nine strokes necessary for learning how to print:

❏ tall straight lines

❏ long straight lines

❏ slanted up lines

❏ slanted down lines

❏ circles

❏ left ear strokes

❏ right ear strokes

❏ smiling strokes

❏ frowning strokes

2. Student has mastered the ability to draw the following shapes:

❏ square

❏ rectangle

❏ triangle

❏ rhombus

❏ circle

❏ oval

3. Student is able to print the following letters:

tall and long straight lines

❏ I
❏ i
❏ L
❏ T
❏ t
❏ F
❏ E
❏ H
❏ l

slanted lines

❏ V
❏ v
❏ W
❏ w
❏ N
❏ M
❏ Z
❏ z
❏ X
❏ x
❏ A
❏ Y
❏ y
❏ K
❏ k

circles

❏ O
❏ o
❏ Q

left ear curves

❏ C
❏ c
❏ G
❏ e
❏ a
❏ d
❏ g
❏ q

right ear curves

❏ D
❏ P
❏ R
❏ B
❏ p
❏ b

left and right ear curves

❏ S
❏ s

smiling curves

❏ U
❏ u
❏ J
❏ j

frowning curves

❏ n
❏ m
❏ r
❏ h
❏ f

Let's learn how to draw a tall straight line.

Directions: Start at each " • " and draw a tall straight line.

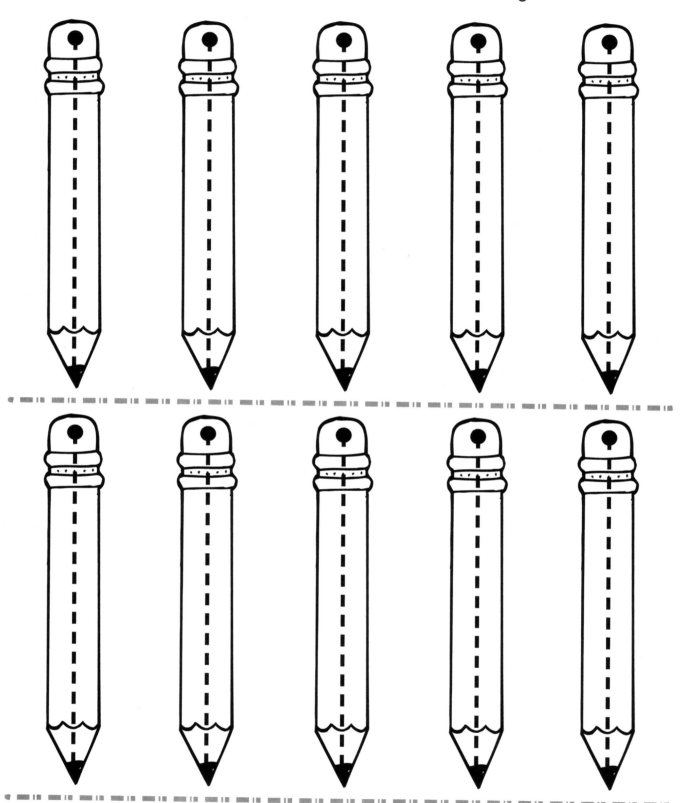

Color Crayons

Directions: Start at each "•" and draw tall straight lines.

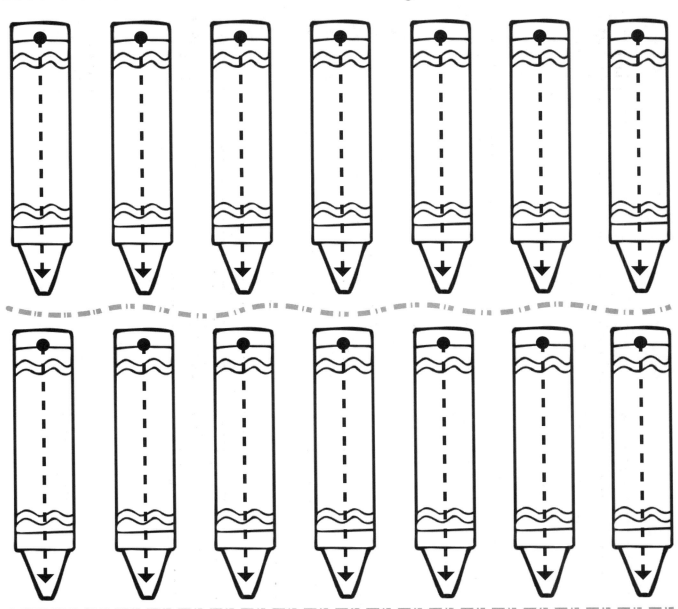

Now you can print the letter " | ."

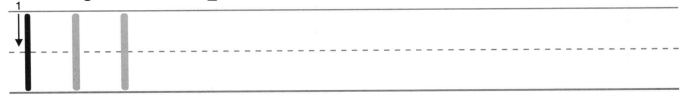

Match the "Same" Pictures

Directions: Start at each "•" and draw tall straight lines.

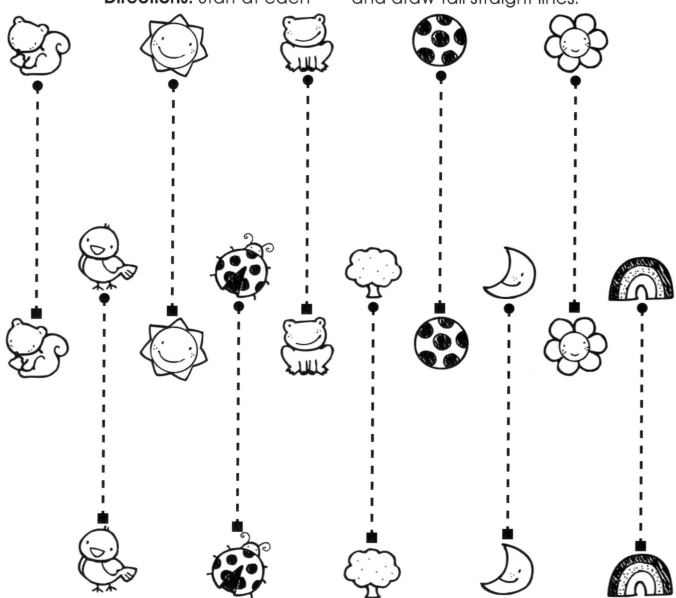

Now you can print the letter "i."

Let's learn how to draw a long straight line.

Directions: Trace the dotted lines to draw long straight lines. Color the picture.

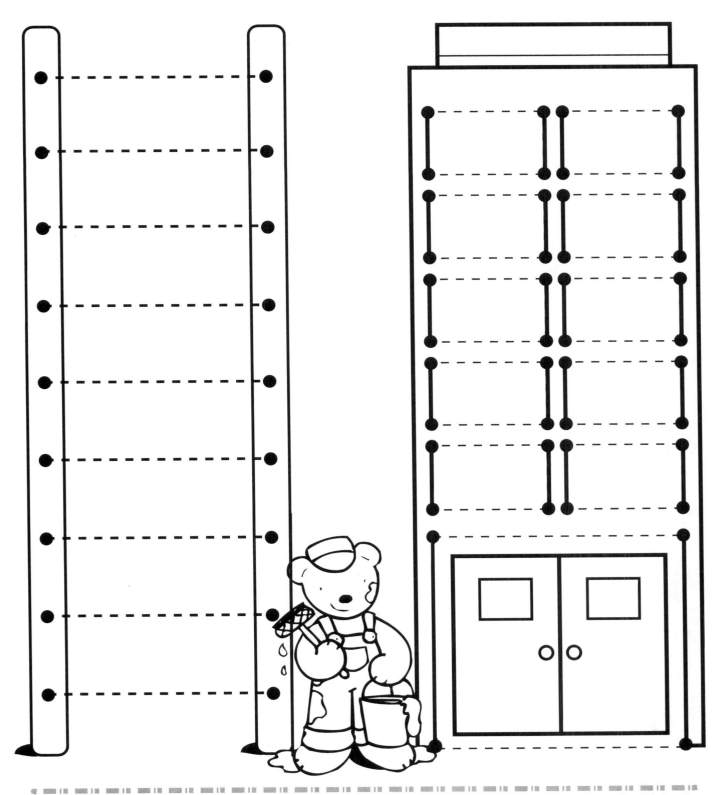

Help the Cat Get Back Home!

Directions: Help the cat find her home.
Start at the " • " and draw tall and long straight lines.

Now you can print the letters " L and T ."

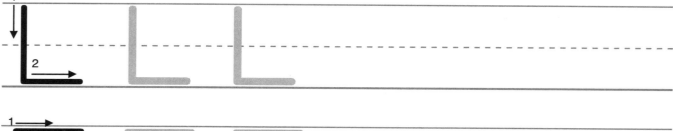

Kites in the Sky

Directions: Draw lines to finish the kites. Color the picture.

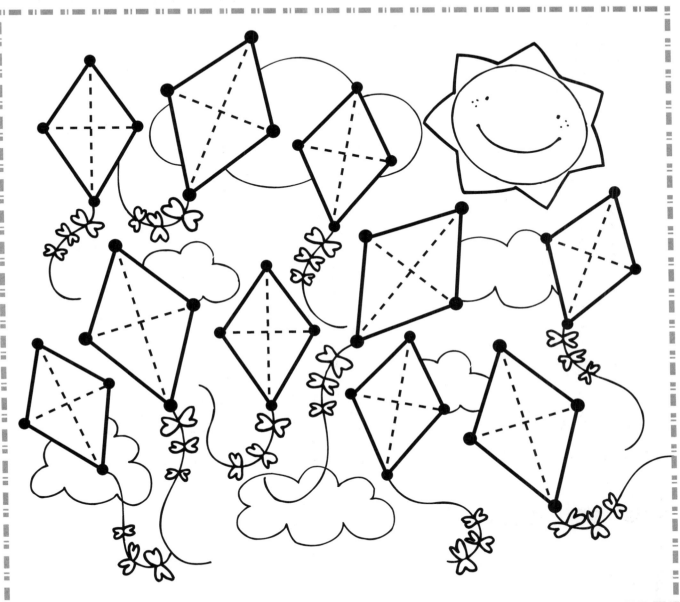

Now you can print the letter " † ."

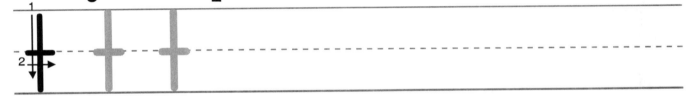

Dot-to-Dot City

Directions: Start at number " I.• " and draw tall and long straight lines. Color the picture.

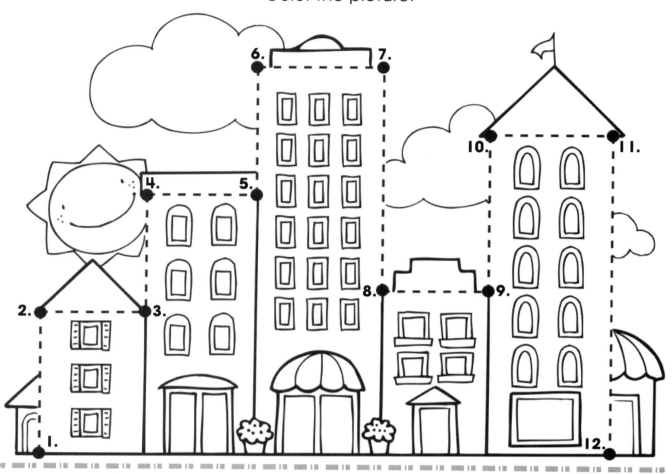

Now you can print the letters " F and E ."

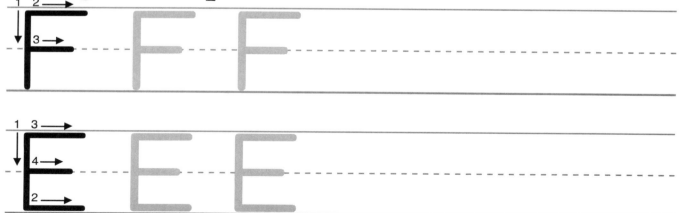

Copy Cat Letters

Directions: Be a copy cat. Trace and then print the letters.

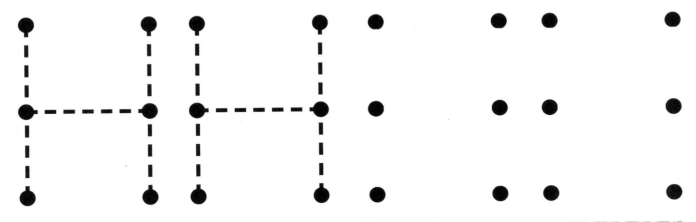

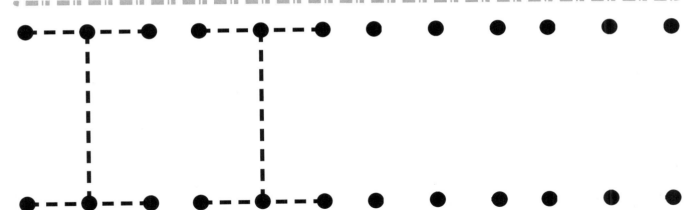

Now you can print the letters " H and I ."

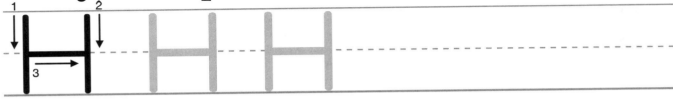

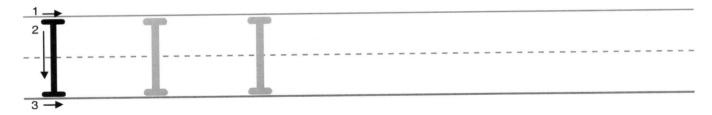

Graphing Picture House

Directions: Look at the example. Draw the house on the blank grid.

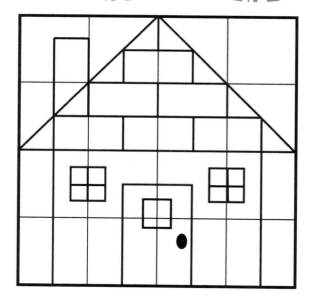

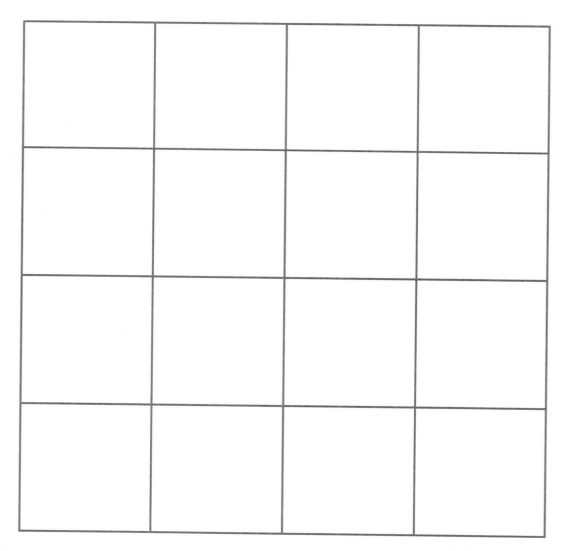

Name _____

Trace and Color Squares

Directions: Trace and color the squares.

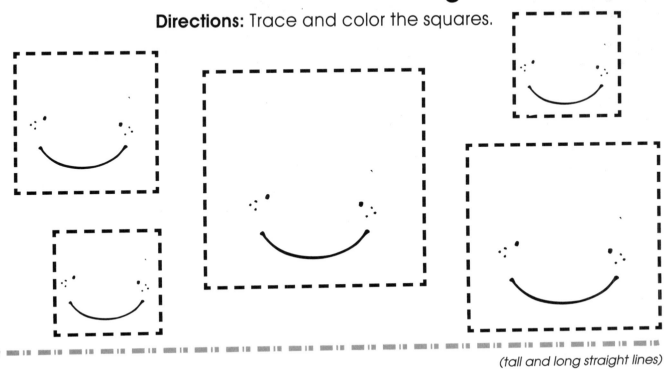

Name _____

Directions: Connect the " • 's" to make squares.

Draw Squares

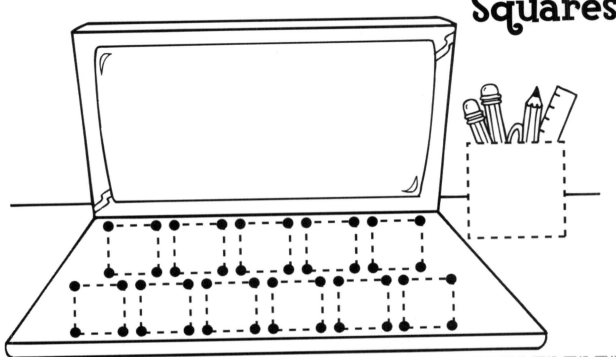

Name _____

Trace and Color Rectangles

Directions: Trace and color the rectangles.

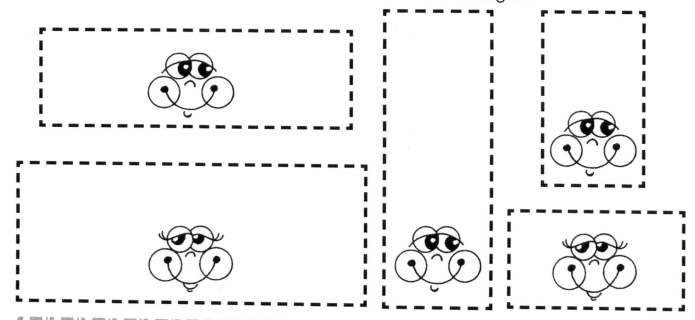

Name _____

Draw Rectangles

Directions: Connect the " • 's" to make rectangles.

Let's learn how to draw an "up" slanted line.

Directions: Start at each " • " and draw "up" slanted lines.

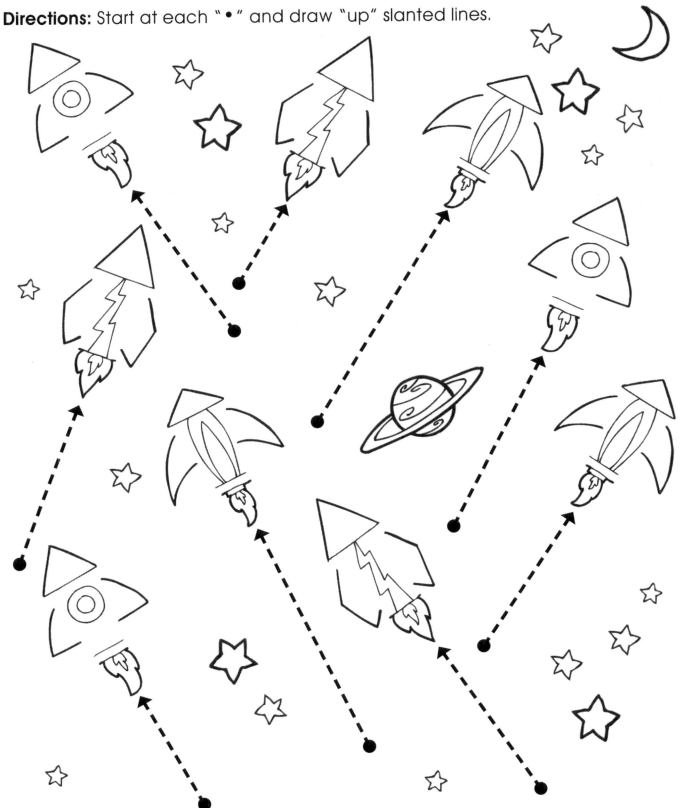

Let's learn how to draw a "down" slanted line.

Directions: Start at each " • " and draw "down" slanted lines.

Finish the Feathers

Directions: Start at each "•" and trace the slanted lines.

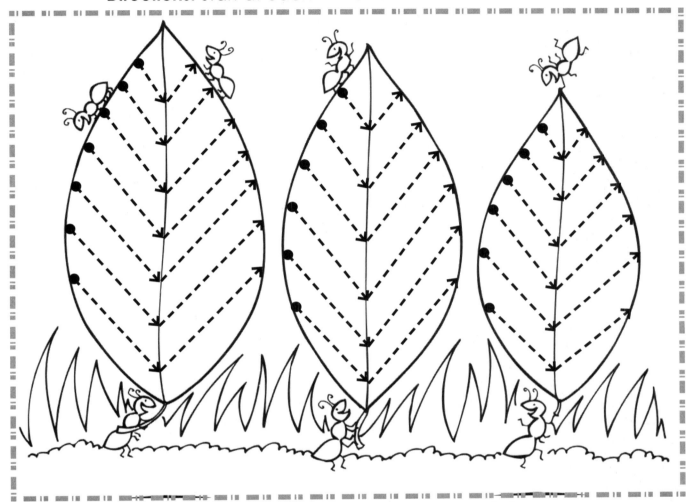

Now you can print the letters " V and v ."

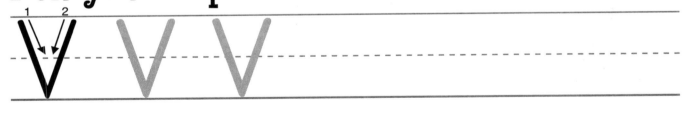

Finish the Picture

Directions: Look at the example.
Draw lines to make your hot air balloon look the same.

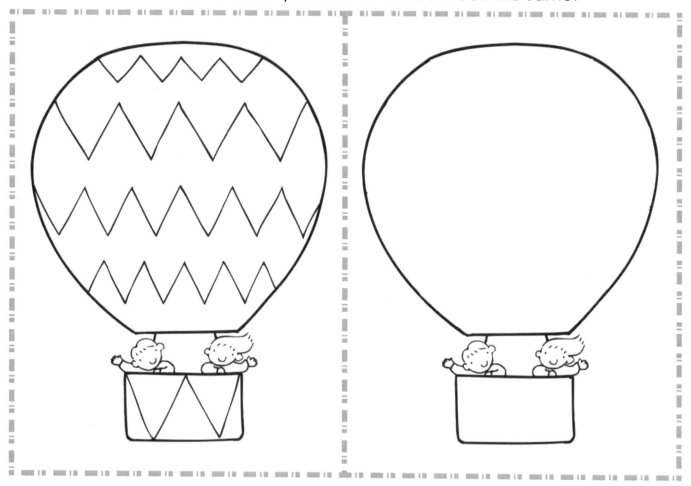

Now you can print the letters " W and w ."

Help the Bird Get to Her Nest

Directions: Draw down and up slanted lines. Color the picture.

Now you can print the letter " N ."

The Mountain Man

Directions: Connect the " • 's" to get the man over the mountains and color.

Now you can print the letter " M ."

Zig-Zag Goals!

Directions: Trace the lines to get the soccer players to the correct goals.

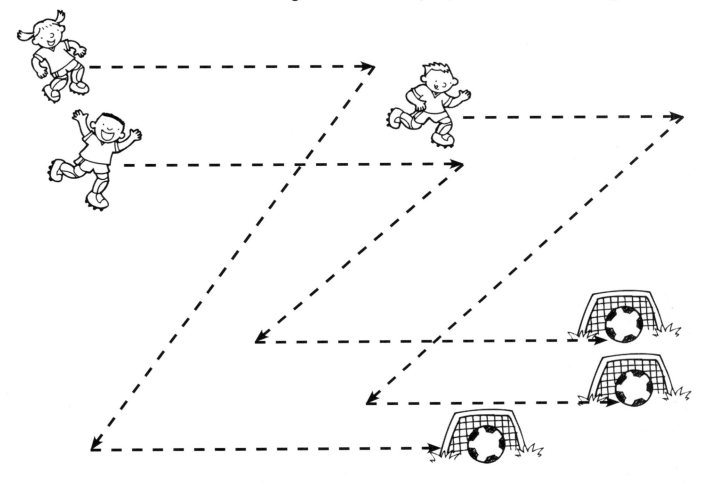

Now you can print the letters " Z and z ."

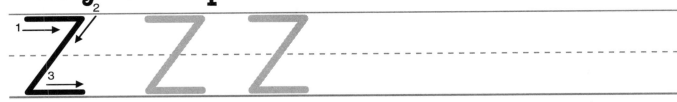

My Own Tree House

Directions: Draw a tree house using tall, long, and slanted lines.

Snowflakes

Directions: Connect the " • 's" to make snowflakes.

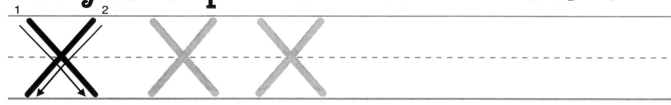

Now you can print the letters " X and x ."

Party Hats

Directions: Connect the " • 's" to make party hats. Color the hats.

Now you can print the letter " A ."

"Y" Guys

Directions: Connect the " • 's" to make the "Y" Guys. Color the guys.

Now you can print the letters " y and Y ."

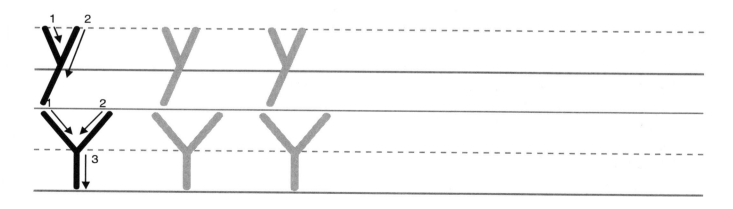

Singing Chicks

Directions: Connect the "•'s" to make the chicks. Color the chicks.

Now you can print the letters " K and k ."

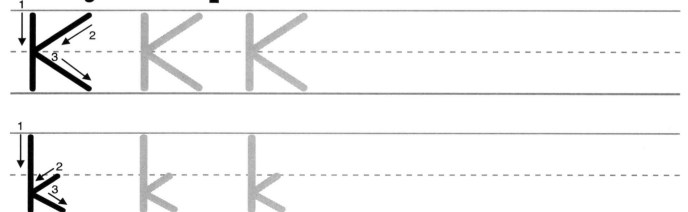

 28 *Pre-Printing Fun*

Graphing Picture Castle

Directions: Look at the example. Draw the castle on the blank grid. Use tall, long, and slanted lines.

Name _____

Trace and Color Triangles

Directions: Trace and color the triangles.

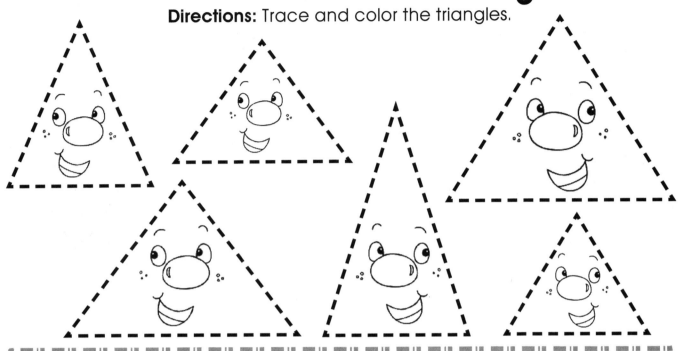

Name _____

Draw Triangles

Directions: Connect the "•'s" to make triangles.

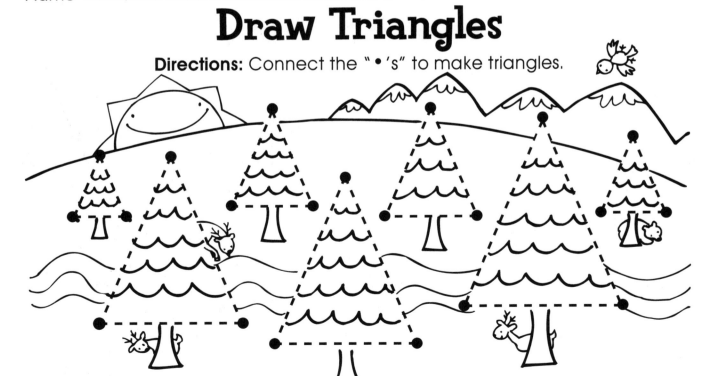

Name _____

Trace and Color Rhombus'

Directions: Trace and color each rhombus.

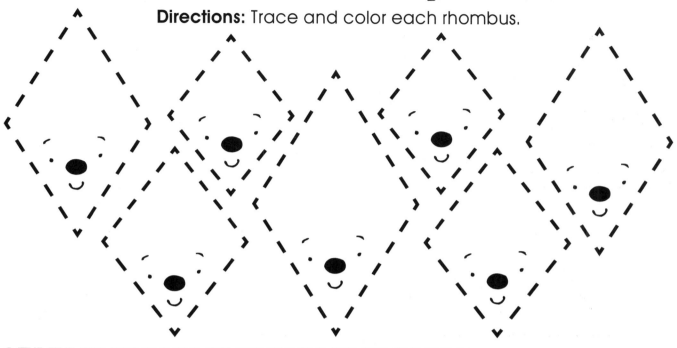

Name _____

Draw Rhombus'

Directions: Connect the " • 's" to make rhombus'.

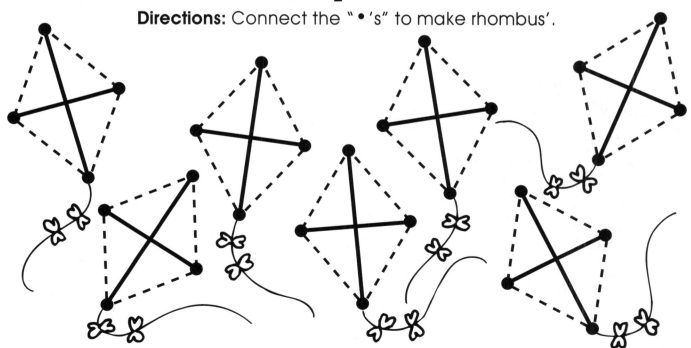

Let's learn how to draw a circle.

Directions: Trace the circles on the pizza. Color the picture.

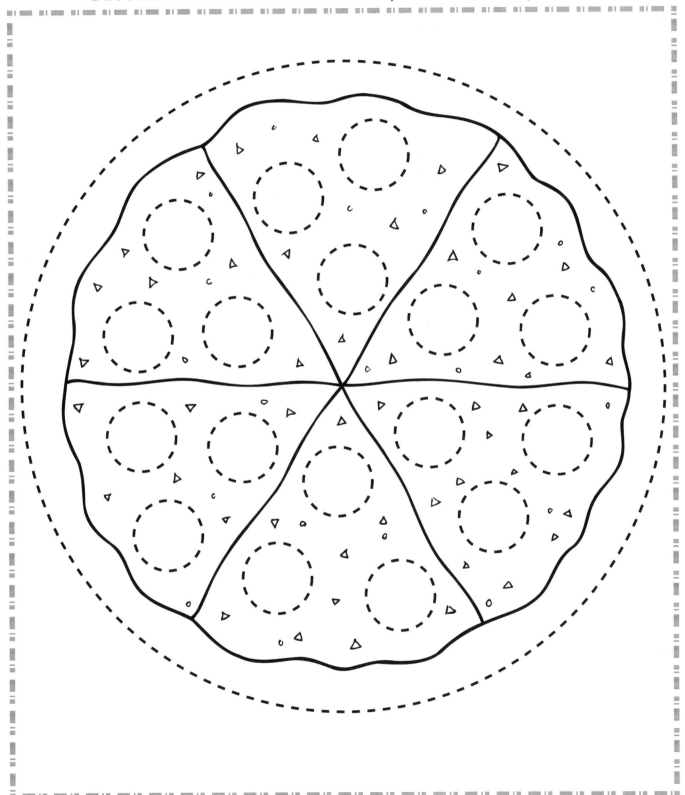

Blowing Bubbles

Directions: Draw your own bubbles.

Now you can print the letters " ◯ and ∘ ."

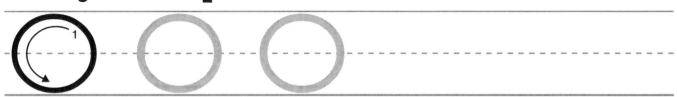

Barnyard Chicks

Directions: Trace and color the chicks.

Now you can print the letter " Q ."

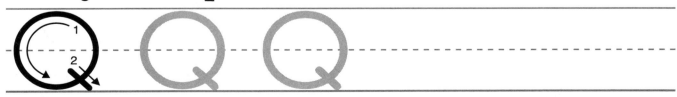

Name _____

Trace and Color Circles

Directions: Trace and color the circles.
Draw and color black circle ears.

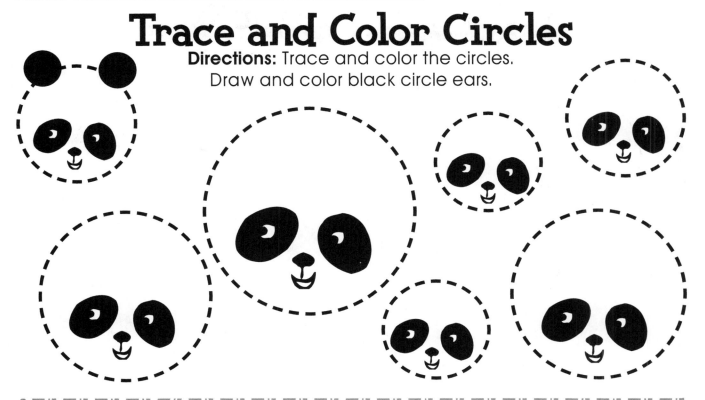

Name _____

Draw Circles

Directions: Draw circles
on the dinosaur.

Name _____

Trace and Color Ovals

Directions: Trace and color the ovals.

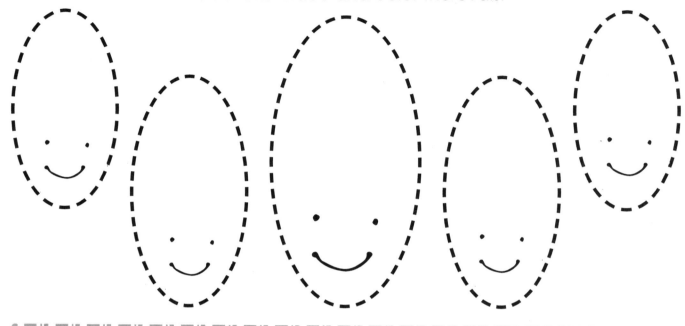

Name _____

Draw Ovals

Directions: Draw ovals to finish the mirrors.

Pre-Printing Fun

Cut and Paste Puzzle

Directions: Cut out the picture squares below.
Glue them on the grid to make a picture.

glue	glue	glue
glue	glue	glue

Let's learn how to draw a left ear stroke.

Directions: Start at the "•" and trace the left ear strokes.

Finish the Animals

Directions: Trace the left ear curves to finish the animals.

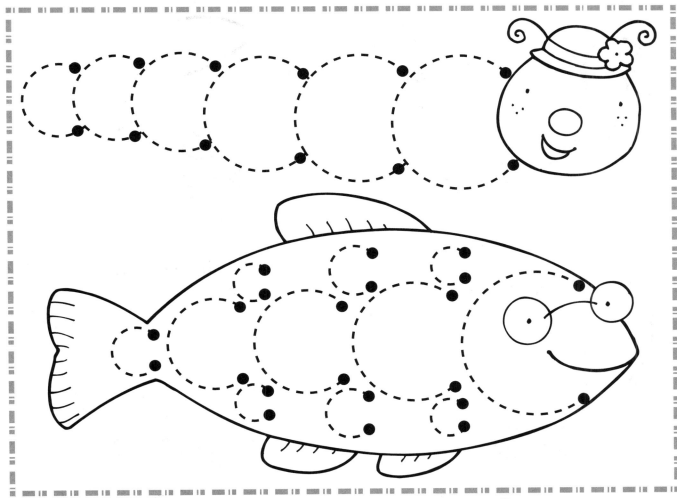

Now you can print the letters " C and c ."

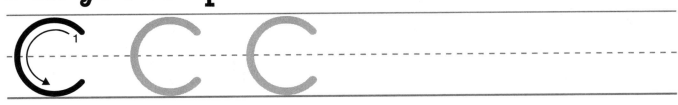

Leaping Lily Pads!

Directions: Trace the left ear curves to finish the lily pads. Color the picture.

Now you can print the letter " G."

Ladybugs Everywhere!

Directions: Trace the left ear curves to finish the ladybugs. Color the picture.

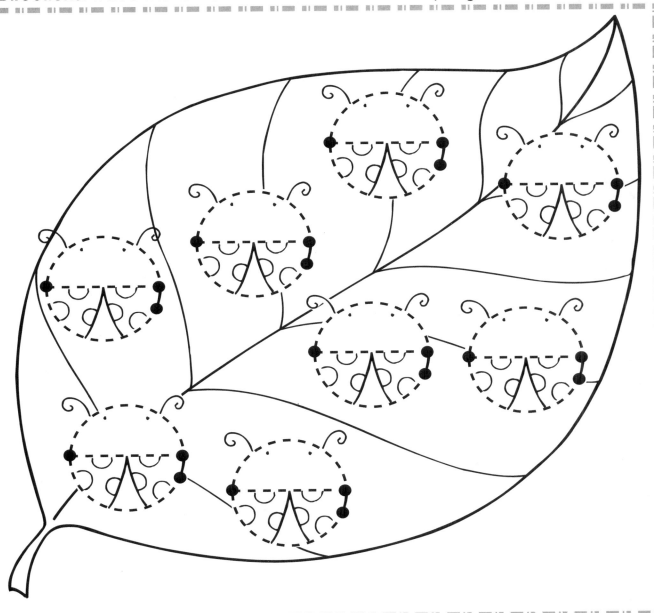

Now you can print the letter " e ."

Long and Short Legs

Directions: Draw left ear curves to finish the animals' legs. Color the animals.

Now you can print the letters " a and d ."

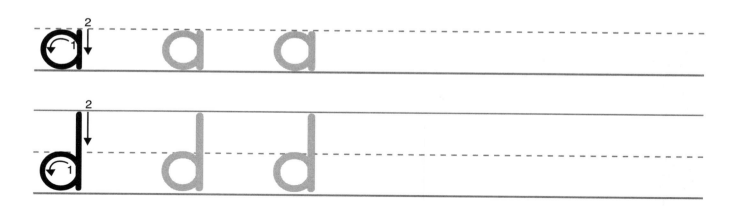

Kittens and Yarn

Directions: Trace the lines to the yarn for each kitten. Color the kittens.

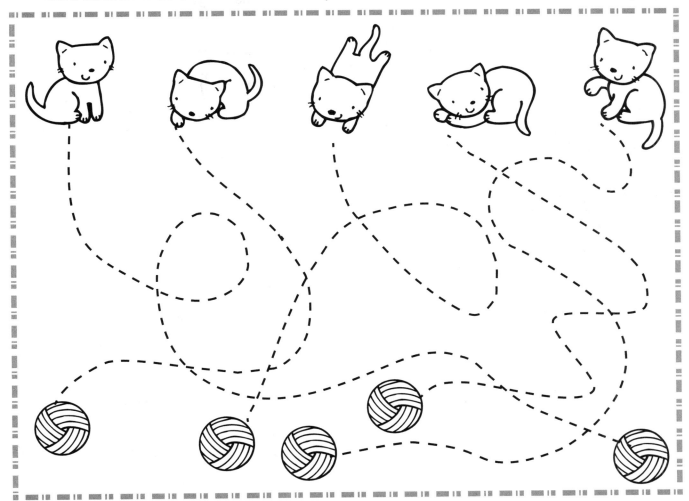

Now you can print the letters " g and q."

Finish the Picture

Directions: Use left ear curves to finish the butterfly. Color the picture.

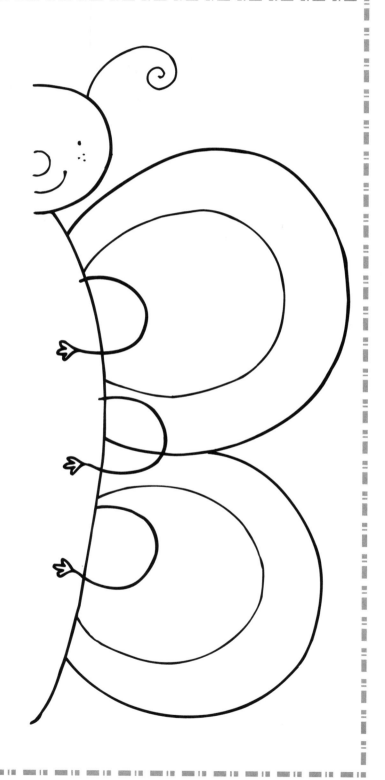

Let's learn how to draw a right ear stroke.

Directions: Start at the "•" and trace the right ear strokes. Color the picture.

Under the Sea

Directions: Trace the right ear curves to finish the pictures. Color the picture.

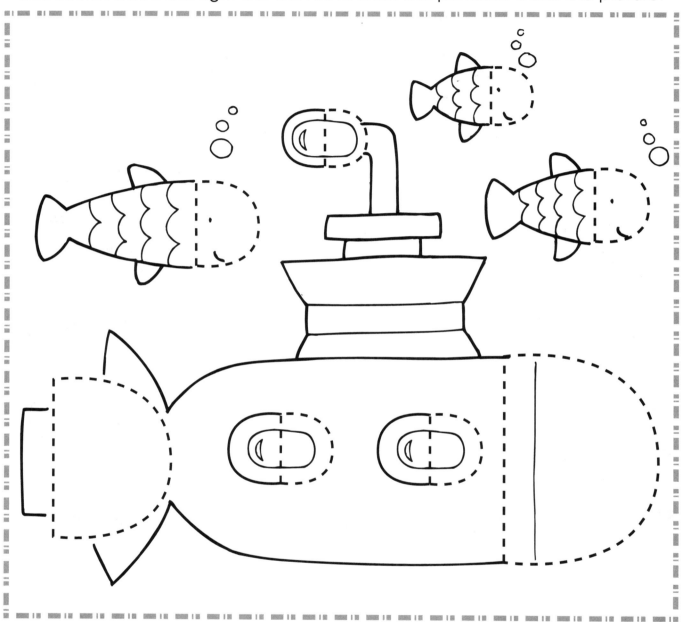

Now you can print the letter " D ."

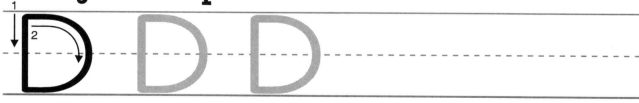

Penguin's Hidden Pictures

Directions: Look at the picture. Find all the "P's and R's."
Trace each letter with a blue crayon.

Now you can print the letters " P and R ."

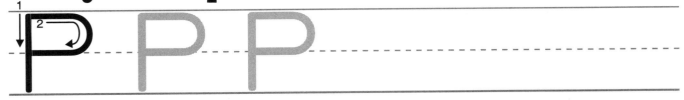

Following Directions

Directions: Look at the directions. Draw and color your own butterfly.

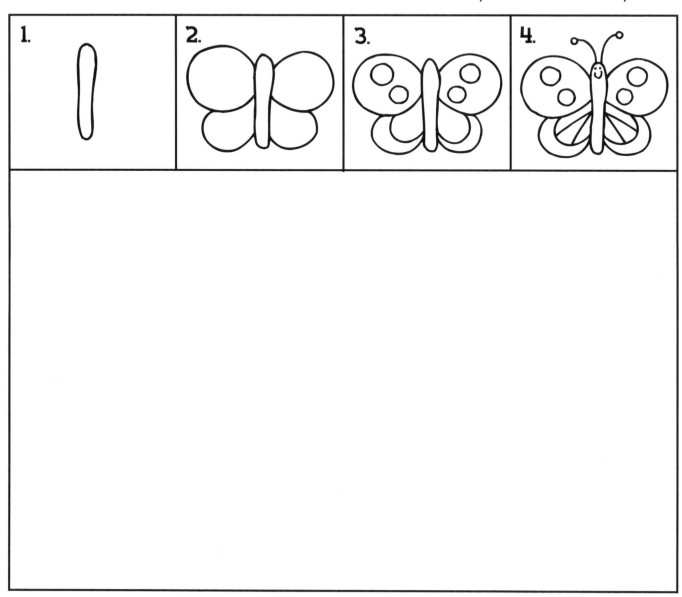

1.

2.

3.

4.

Now you can print the letter " B ."

Directions:

Trace the dotted lines to finish the owl.

Can you see a "**b**" and a "**p**"?

Finish the Owl

Now you can print the letters " p and b ."

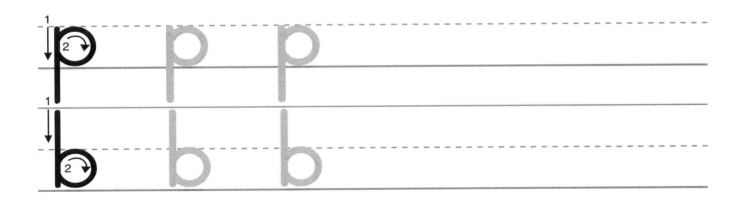

Trace and Dot-to-Dot

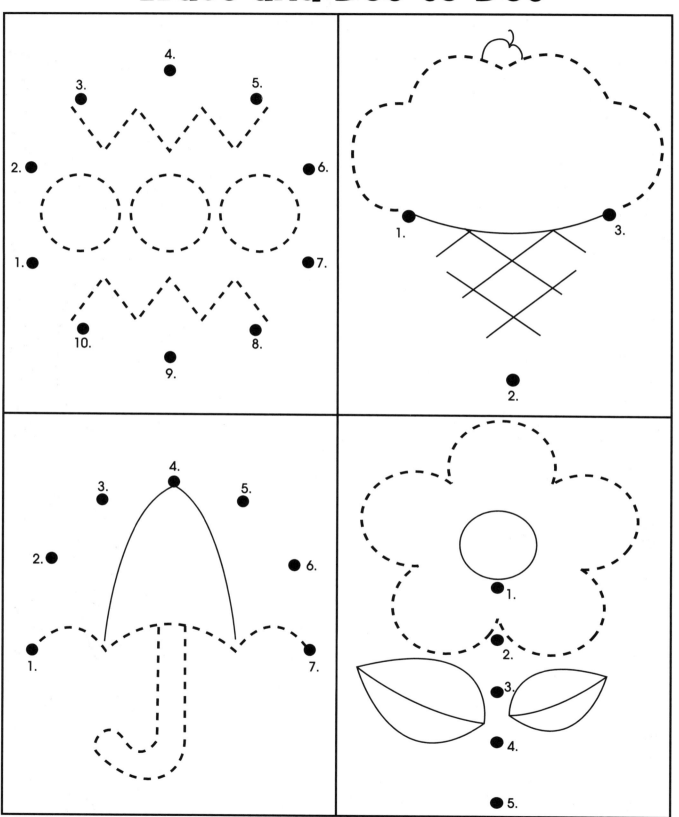

Slithering Snakes

Directions: Start at each "•" and draw curves.

Flamingos

Directions: Trace the left and right ear curves. Color the flamingos.

Now you can print the letters " S and s."

Let's learn how to draw a smile stroke.

Directions: Start at the " • " and trace all the smile strokes. Color the children.

The Wavy Ocean

Directions: Trace smile curves to finish the ocean. Color the picture.

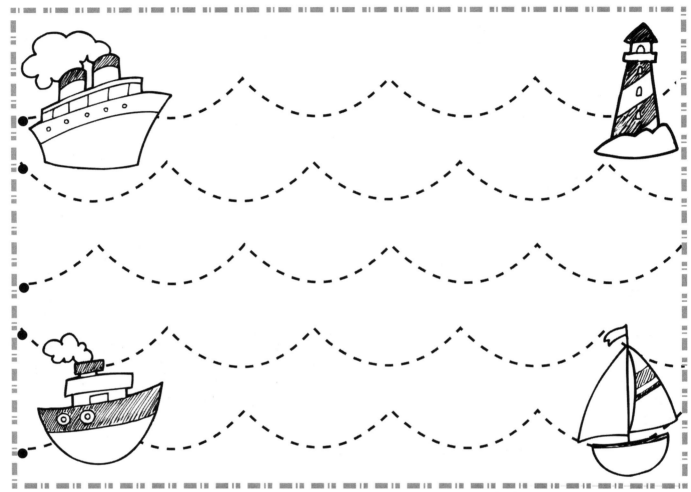

Now you can print the letters " U and u ."

Cute Cottage Dot-to-Dot

Directions: Trace smile curves and connect the dots to finish the cottage.

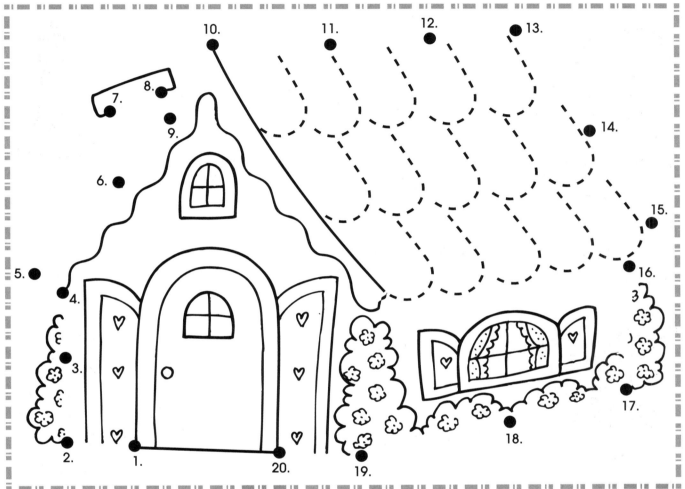

Now you can print the letters " J and j."

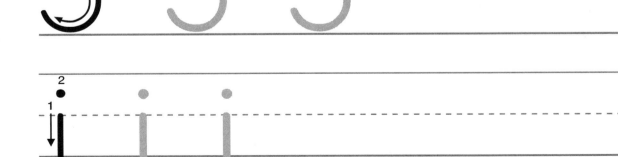

Flower Garden

Directions: Trace the curves to finish the flowers. Color the picture.

Let's learn how to draw a frown stroke.

Directions: Start at the " • " and trace all the frown strokes. Color the children.

Everyone frowns sometimes!

Directions: Draw a picture of what you look like when you are sad.

Hopping Critters

Directions: Trace the frown curves. Color the animals.

Now you can print the letters " n and m ."

Following Directions

Directions: Look at the directions. Draw and color your own sheep.

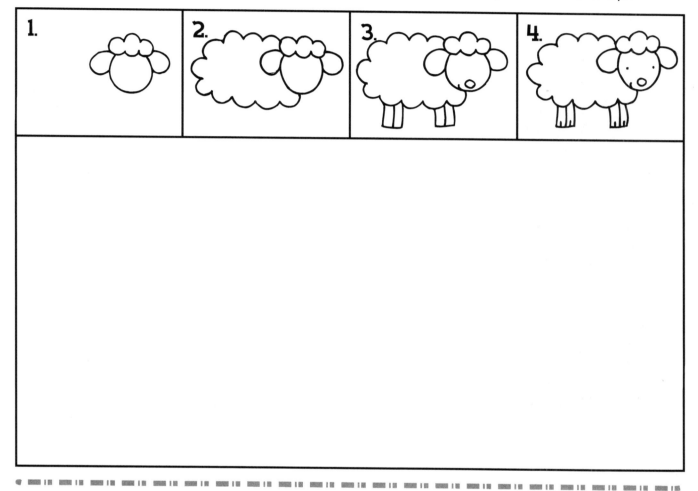

Now you can print the letters " r and h ."

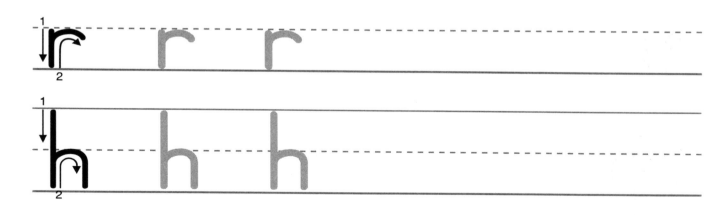

Name _____

Puppy's Hidden Picture

Directions: Look at the picture. Find all the "f's."
Trace each "f" with a red crayon.

Now you can print the letter " f ."

A Tricky Maze

Directions: Help the monkey get his bananas.
Use straight and curved lines to get through the maze.

Finish the Peacock

Directions: Draw some more feathers for the peacock. Color the peacock.

Name _____

Practice Printing the Alphabet

Directions: Trace the letters. Print them all by yourself on the back of the paper.

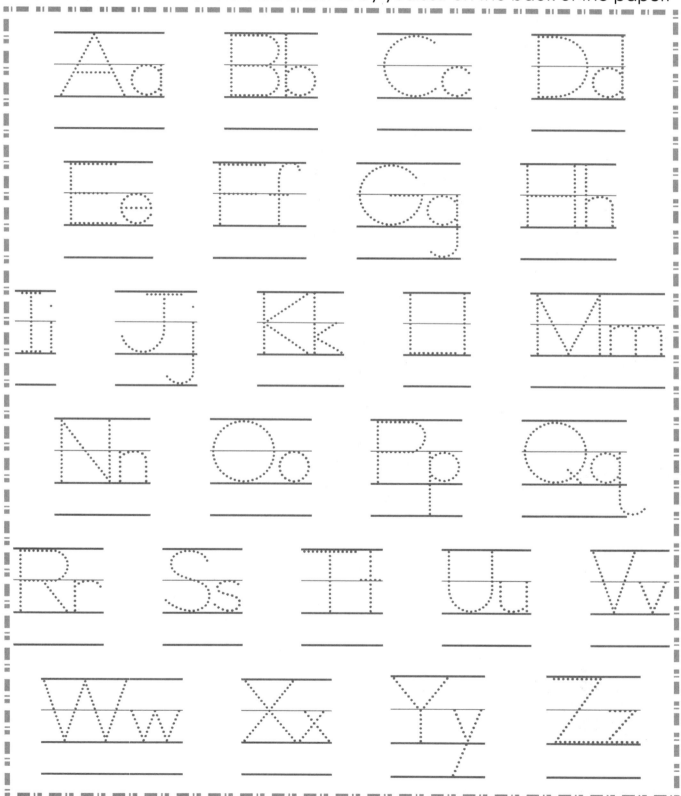

Standards Correlation

Pre-Printing FUN
Developmentally-Appropriate Activities that will Strengthen Fine Motor Skills, Improve Eye-Hand Coordination, and Increase Pencil Control

This book supports the NCTE/IRA Standards for the English Language Arts and the recommended teaching practices outlined in the NAEYC/IRA position statement Learning to Read and Write: Developmentally Appropriate Practices for Young Children.

NCTE/IRA Standards for the English Language Arts

Each activity in this book supports one or more of the following standards:

1. **Students communicate in spoken, written, and visual form, for a variety of purposes and a variety of audiences.** In *Pre-Printing FUN*, students communicate in visual and written form, by drawing lines and printing letters, to illustrate their progress in learning to write.

NAEYC/IRA Position Statement Learning to Read and Write: Developmentally Appropriate Practices for Young Children

Each activity in this book supports one or more of the following recommended teaching practices for kindergarten and primary students:

1. **Teachers provide opportunities for students to write many different kinds of texts for different purposes.** *Pre-Printing FUN* includes opportunities for students to practice printing letters in order to improve their handwriting skills.

2. **Teachers provide writing experiences that allow children to develop from the use of nonconventional writing forms to the use of more conventional forms.** In *Pre-Printing FUN*, students practice proper letter formation, which allows them to move toward conventional penmanship.